On The Political Position of Social-Democracy by Wilhelm Liebknecht
First Prism Key Press Edition 2011

Prism Key Press
New York, NY 10001
PrismKeyPress.com

ISBN-13: 978-1466378544

On the Political Position of Social-Democracy

Particularly with Respect to the Reichstag
(1869 &1889)

Wilhelm Liebknecht

Contents

PREFACE
TO THE LONDON EDITION OF 1889

Some incorrigible blockheads usually quote this speech – which I am now re-publishing without any changes – to prove that today I am a different person from what I was 19 years ago. Well, I plead guilty and admit forthwith that I am indeed a "conformer" in so far as I act in accordance with circumstances. I even hold the heretic view that a person, who does not modify his actions when circumstances change, will not set the sea on fire. To stick to old tactics when conditions have changed signifies not *a strong character* but *a feeble mind*, not *consistency* but *incompetence*. A general is inept if he is incapable of changing his plan of action in the course of battle; many a brilliant victory has been won by a switch in tactics during the battle.

My *aim* is now the same as it was 20 or 40 or more years ago – merely somewhat clearer and considerably expanded – but I have altered my *tactics* repeatedly, and it is quite possible that I will change them once more or perhaps even several times more. And I will *certainly* do so, if the grounds or basis for it change.

In the first place I would like to draw the reader's attention to *the date* of my speech. It was delivered in 1869, that is, *before the Franco-German War, before the establishment of the German Empire*.

The North German Confederation[1] which then existed, like the queer political formations in Southern Germany, was plainly marked as a transitory phenomenon. Whether it was a *still-birth*, a *miscreation* or the *formation of a new state*, no one could say. Not even Bismarck.[2] For everything depended on *the favourable attitude of foreign countries*, whose *more or less moral support* had helped to bring about this "patriotic" deed.

And I, who *fought* in 1848 and 1849 in the name of German unity and freedom against *the producers of this "national" monstrosity*, who would have been summarily court-martialled had I fallen into their clutches – was I to abandon my past and allow myself to be enticed into the mousetrap of an enlarged Prussian military and police state by the bait of universal suffrage? But that could never be. I saw events then as I should see them now, if the same conditions still prevailed.

The war with France broke out. *The North German Confederation*, which was at the mercy of France and Russia, became *the German Empire*.

That created *a completely new situation*.

In no way does the German Empire correspond to the "national ideal" It embodies neither *unity* nor *freedom*. It is merely a *torso of Germany*, a large barrack enclosed in an even larger prison.

However, the German Empire has *an independent existence*, it is not at the mercy of foreign countries, and it cannot be suddenly overthrown by one blow from within or without. This large barrack, encompassed by a still larger prison, can become a free state only *through internal organic evolution*.

In short, this torso of Germany contains within it the elements that will in time transform it into a really *free and united Germany*, which will occupy an honourable position in *the United States of Europe and of the world*, so that the sorrowful role it now plays in the civilized world will be forgotten.

Were I to follow my wishes and inclination I would never set foot in the *Reichstag*. It always makes me laugh to hear the "anarchist" braggarts call me a dyed-in-the-wool parliamentarian. I am personally at loggerheads with parliamentarism. From time immemorial I have regarded talk and oratory with a certain disdain and I have certainly not been cut out for parliamentary life. It by no means suits my nature. I always speak with reluctance and only because I am compelled by a higher necessity. None can hold a lower opinion than I of my parliamentary accomplishments.

But under prevailing conditions, *parliamentary work* has such great *advantages* for our party, that one must be blind not to appreciate them. It is mainly due to our parliamentary activity and *participation in the elections*, which again is inseparable from arid dependent upon our parliamentary work, that Social-Democracy in Germany is better organized and represents a far greater power than in any other country.

I am fully in accord with my comrades in placing this participation *foremost. The educational results of universal suffrage* are so obvious as to need no re-statement. If we had decided *not to participate* in the elections but to abstain from voting, we would still be *a sect* today and not *a party*, around which the whole of our political life revolves, although all parties-the government included-are most vehemently fighting against us.

That *propaganda* is the main purpose of our participation in the elections and in parliamentary work, has been stated so often by my comrades and myself that it needs no further elaboration. So long as we are a small minority, and *all the other parties of the Reichstag confront us as "one reactionary mass,"* which opposes any effective *labour legislation* and any real step towards *social reform*, this cannot change, and to influence the people and win them over to our side will remain the primary purpose of our parliamentary activity.

And now a word about *parliamentarism*. Only a few remarks. Orators are as a rule bad politicians, the orator intoxicates himself and his audience. Rhetorical and histrionic success are similar in so far as they both stimulate *vanity* and produce *a megalomania*, which is usually simply ridiculous but which sometimes can also be dangerous.

Although the principle of *representation* cannot be altogether abandoned, it should however be reduced to a strictly indispensable minimum, in particular, the legislative and government functions should be exercised by *committees* and not by parliament, where, as every experienced person knows, debates are not *serious deliberations* but mere *theatrical performances*. Even today the major work of the Reichstag has to be done in *committees*.

Committees elected by the people for specified purposes, which can *meet* whenever *common interests* are involved, and which have *to submit to plebiscite* all laws before they come into force; *the people possessing* not only *the right to reject*, but also *the right to introduce legislation*; in addition, *complete freedom of the press and of assembly*, and a government which has *no power to wield against the people* – this is, in rough outline, my idea of the future mode of legislation and government – so long as it may still be possible to call it government at all. The government *in the United States of America* is even now to a great extent mere administration, and it will become exclusively administration as soon as *the class rule of the bourgeoisie* is smashed, for the latter *must furnish the state or the government with the power to oppress the working people*.

However, this is for the time being only a "dream of the future." For *the present* I have defined in a speech, is which I also delivered a few years ago in Berlin, my parliamentary or non-parliamentary programme as follows:

The greatest possible restriction of rhetorical aspects, speeches to be made only when required by party interests. If these are not involved, e.g., if it is not a matter of *labour legislation*, or *branding the enemy, evaluation of prevailing conditions*, and if no *propagandist task* is served-silence is better than talk, *prolific* and *eloquent talk* spells death to *vigorous action*, and has become the *grave of many a party*.

Parliamentary activity ought to be restricted to bare

necessity, not only at plenary sessions of the Reichstag, but also in the committees, if these are again opened to us. But only *restricted*, for it would be just as foolish *to renounce* the weapons which we obtain through our participation in committee meetings as to exclude ourselves from the legislative work at the plenary sessions. Our electors justly demand that we *do our utmost* in the Reichstag *to improve the position of the working people* and *to advance the cause of Social-Democracy.* To assume a purely negative or dissenting attitude would be the surest way of alienating our voters and cutting the ground from under our feet. Here again, as usual in practical politics, the simple *utilitarian point of view is decisive – provided the inviolability of principle is maintained.*

Borsdorf, November 15, 1888
W. Liebknecht

PREFACE
TO THE SECOND EDITION

What I was compelled to say with regard to the following speech during the recent proceedings of the "high treason trial"[3] at the Leipzig Jury Court, makes a detailed explanation now superfluous. I have only little to add. The address, delivered fully three years ago, was a "topical speech" and has to be understood as such. I need neither withdraw nor qualify anything. Least of all my criticism of Bismarck's parliamentarism, which is manifesting itself as gloriously in the "*German* Reichstag" as in the quondam "*North German* Reichstag."

In fact I should rather have extended my censure of this particular excrescence to *parliamentarism as a whole*. For though it has played nowhere – not even in the *Bas-Empire* of Bonaparte – such a melancholy role as in Prussian Germany, it helps to deceive and enslave the people in *all* countries where it prevails; behind this opera-cloak, adorned with the tinsel of empty phrases, absolutism and class rule hide their ugly limbs and their murderous weapons. Where the people govern, in Switzerland and in America – although they are not model republics in the Social-Democratic sense – there is no parliamentarism. Direct government and legislation by the people, which is our aim, will not be able to dispense altogether with a representative body, but the delegates, brought to the fore by the people's *free* choice, will form *committees*, designed to discharge certain, clearly defined tasks; but not gossip clubs where verbose impotence flourishes and where conscientious investigation, serious debate, and resolute decisions are quite impossible. It was not the French *Convention* but its *committees* which accomplished the gigantic task facing the militant revolution-the cleansing of the Augean stables[4] of feudal society. Even our parliament is forced to let committees transact

13

its real business. But I will deal with that on another occasion.

Because of the party relations prevailing at that time, I still distinguished in my speech between Schweitzer's activity and the royal Prussian court socialism. Bebel's[5] address and mine at the general meeting of the General Association of German Workers,[6] held at Barmen-Elberfeld in March 1869, had brought about a sort of truce with Herr van Schweitzer[7] which then still obtained, though it lapsed *soon* afterwards. However strong Schweitzer's influence on the General Association of German Workers was and, I regret to say, indirectly still is at the present time, I have never identified Herr von Schweitzer – now happily advanced to Poet Laureate – with this Association, whose political position could be correctly described in those days as "national-liberal."

The emphasis which I put on the indivisibility of democracy and socialism was called forth by Schweitzer's tactics of arousing doubts about democracy among the workers; and all the misinterpretations of "bourgeois democracy," which I defended against the Jesuitical attacks of the royal Prussian Socialists, have now lost their grounds because of *Jacoby's*[8] *joining the Social-Democratic Party*, for I had in mind only Jacoby and his associates.

After these preliminary remarks, I let my speech follow unchanged according to the version published in summer 1869 in the **Demokratisches Wochenblatt**[9] and later on in pamphlet form; a version incidentally that was *not* based on a stenographic report.

ON THE POLITICAL POSITION OF SOCIAL-DEMOCRACY

Particularly with Respect to the North German Reichstag

(1869)

Since I was unable to take the floor in the Reichstag this time, I have with particular pleasure availed myself of this opportunity to state my social and political views.

The question as to what position Social-Democracy should occupy in the political fight, can be answered easily and confidently if we clearly understand that *socialism and democracy are inseparable*. Socialism and democracy are not identical, but they are simply different expressions of the same principle; they belong together, supplement each other, and *one can never be incompatible with the other*. Socialism without democracy is pseudo-socialism, just as democracy without socialism is pseudo-democracy. *The democratic state is the only feasible form for a society organized on a socialist basis.*

All enemies of the bourgeoisie agree with the negative aspect of socialism. *Wagener*[10] and *Bishop Ketteller*[11], the Catholic clergy in the Austrian Reichsrat, the Protestant squires of the Prussian model state – they all condemn the bourgeoisie just as loudly as the most radical Socialist, using the same slogans. This shows that in itself the fight against the bourgeoisie is not necessarily democratic, but can arise from the most reactionary motives. Here we are faced immediately with the necessity of emphasizing not only the negative side of socialism but also its positive side, which distinguishes us from those reactionaries; and, above all, of waging a *political* fight in addition to the social fight, and of *marching in its front ranks* at that. We call ourselves *Social-Democrats*, because we have understood that democracy and socialism are inseparable. Our programme is implied in this name. But a programme is not designed to be given merely lip-service and to be repudiated in action. It should be the standard which determines our conduct.

If we restrict ourselves to the social struggle, or pay insufficient attention to the political battles, we run the risk that our enemies will make use of the existing class antagonisms, and in accordance with the maxim *divide et impera* flirt sometimes with the bourgeoisie against the workers, sometimes with the workers against the bourgeoisie. *This kind of double-dealing is typical of modern Caesarism, which is based essentially on the exploitation of class antagonisms.* In *France* the Empire today "saves" the bourgeoisie from the workers, and tomorrow it flirts with the workers, to drive the frightened bourgeoisie into its net. Here in *Prussia*, Caesarism copies its French model also in this respect, and alternately pats the bourgeoisie and the workers on the shoulder. Thus it happened that National-Liberalism, that is, the political party representing the bourgeoisie, looks towards the government for its salvation from the workers, while deluded workers – I hope not many despite the systematic corruption from the top – expect the same government to give them protection against the bourgeoisie.

If Caesarism is not to benefit from the social movement, socialism must take the lead in the political struggle.

Above all one thing must be clearly stated: the social movement is a process of revolutionary transformation, which cannot be accomplished overnight. The social question does not resemble that mythical plant whose buds suddenly burst into flower after lying dormant for a century. The word "revolution" expresses two different things. Sometimes it means simply the overthrow of a government, which can be the result of a brief street battle. That is the narrower sense of the word. In the wider sense it comprises the entire development of a new social structure, which has to create for itself an adequate political form. And although *this* revolutionary process, which continues even during the most calm periods, can be accelerated, it cannot be compressed at will by a magic formula into an arbitrarily chosen minimum length of time.

The bourgeoisie required half a millennium to develop its present power. The proletariat, which must abolish the bourgeois method of production based on the wage system and eradicate class rule together with wage slavery, cannot solve its task in a few years. But the modern proletarian revolution will not take as long as the bourgeois revolution did – in the age of the steam-engine and the telegraph, humanity advances more rapidly, culture is made accessible to a greater number of people, and the army fighting for the new ideas has a wider recruitment field.

But the new society is in irreconcilable contradiction to the old state. It cannot develop in the feudal, police and military state. *Whoever wants the new society, therefore has to aim at the destruction of the old state*. That is why, under present conditions, Social-Democracy is restricted mainly to the field of *theory* in so far as the purely social question is concerned. *It has yet to win the political basis* for its *social practice*.

This determines the attitude of Social-Democracy towards "Germany's reorganization." The "action" of 1866 is for Germany, what the *coup d'etat* of December 2, 1851 was for France. Bismarck's *coup d'etat*, like that of Louis Napoleon, was aimed against democracy. It is not *the use of force* in these acts, which causes us to condemn them – since force is the last resort of both sovereigns and nations – but that they were perpetrated in France for the benefit of a crowd of depraved adventurers, and in Germany for the benefit of a class that has no longer any right to exist, the Junkers, the landed aristocracy.

The so-called "Prussian *constitutional conflict*"[12] was an attempt by the people, in the first place the bourgeoisie, to gain state power by *parliamentary* means. The year 1866 has degraded the parliamentary struggle to a sham fight and transferred the real scene of action to another sphere. In spite of universal suffrage the North German "Reichstag" has absolutely no power, having no determining but only an advisory capacity, and because it is without power it cannot serve democracy as a battle-ground for *the attainment of power.*

Just as French democracy stood against the Empire, so German democracy must repudiate and oppose the North German Confederation and all its appurtenances. If it were to relinquish this opposition, it would not only surrender its principle and therefore itself, but also violate the simplest rules of practical action.

Now to the question: should democracy participate at all in the elections to the "Reichstag"? To vote or not to vote is merely a question of *expediency,* not a question of principle, where universal suffrage exists. We have the *right* to vote – the fact that the right has been thrust upon us does not deprive us of our natural right – and when we can *benefit* by it, we vote. It is from this point of view that we in Saxony considered the convocation of the "Reichstag." For reasons of expediency some were against, others for participation in the election. Those favouring abstention declared that this course would help to bring home to the people the absence of civil rights, while those favouring participation emphasized, that if democracy were to abstain our opponents would gain exclusive possession of the speaker's platform, that they alone would hold the floor, and could thus all the more readily confuse the people's sense of justice. This consideration prevailed, and it was decided to take part in the election. My personal opinion was that the representatives elected by us should enter the "Reichstag," deliver their protest, and depart again immediately afterwards, without however resigning their seats. I remained in the minority with that opinion; it was agreed that the representatives of democracy could make use of any opportunity that appeared practical to them to voice their opposition and their protest in the "Reichstag," but that they keep aloof from parliamentary business proper, for this would imply recognition of the North German Confederation and Bismarck's policy, and could only mislead the people about the fact that *the fight in the "Reichstag" is merely a sham fight, merely a comedy*. We followed this rule in the first and second session of the "Reichstag." During the debate on *trade regulations*, which formed the main subject of the present session, some of my party comrades thought that in the interest of the workers and for propaganda purposes they had to make an exception. I did not agree. Under no circumstances and on no grounds should the Social-Democratic Party negotiate with its adversaries. *One can only negotiate where a common basis exists*. To negotiate with an opponent from whom one differs in matters of principle amounts to a sacrifice of principle. Principles are indivisible, they can either be *maintained completely* or *sacrificed completely*. The smallest concession on a point of principle is a renunciation of the principle. Those who converse with the enemy parley, those who parley come to terms.

The Progressive Party[13] (*Fortschrittspartei*) can serve as an instructive and cautionary example. At the time of the so-called Prussian constitutional conflict it spared no pains to deliver beautiful as well as strong speeches. How energetically it protested against the reorganization – in words! How "staunchly" and "ably" it championed the rights of the people – in words! But the government took no notice of these legal deductions. Yielding the right to the Progressive Party, it retained and used the power. And the Progressive Party? Instead of abandoning the parliamentary fight, which under the circumstances had become harmful tomfoolery, instead of withdrawing from the speaker's rostrum, thus compelling the government to reveal its naked absolutism, instead of appealing to the people, the Progressive Party, taking satisfaction from its own phrases, continued untiringly to issue empty protests and legal conclusions and to pass resolutions which were bound to remain ineffective, as everybody knew. Thus the Chamber of Deputies was transformed from a political arena into a theatre.

Hearing always the same speeches and seeing always the same lack of results, the people turned away, at first with indifference and then with disgust. *The year 1866 thus became possible*. The "beautiful" "strong" opposition speeches of the Prussian Progressive Party prepared the ground for the blood and iron policy,[14] *they were the funeral orations of the Progressive Party itself. In the most literal sense of the word it had talked itself to death.*

Lassalle[15], I must recall here, and I would like to remind in particular those members of the Association founded by him who may be present – Lassalle condemned most emphatically the conduct of the Progressive Party and predicted the consequences. He advised the deputies to withdraw from the parliamentary scene and to resign their seats. But unfortunately he did not go so far as to demand that they *refuse* to vote for *the finance bills*, at that time the only way, and a sure way, of keeping the government in check. However that may be, Lassalle in any case showed clearly the perversity and the ruinous effect of parliamentary rhetoric, of talking for the sake of talking.

If democracy now commits the same error as the Progressive Party committed six years ago, the same cause will again produce the same effect.

But quite apart from the strictly political point of view, our party's participation in parliamentary debates cannot be of the slightest practical use.

It will be readily granted that with the present composition of the Reichstag it is quite impossible to carry any motions which are fundamentally important from our point of view.

"But," some may argue, "in the Reichstag we have the best opportunity to expound Social-Democratic principles." Of course there is that opportunity; but certainly not the best, and not even a good one.

Do you believe the "Reichstag" will permit us to use its floor as *a speaker's platform*? Suppose a person like Marx wished to deliver a series of theoretical lectures to the deputies, how long, and how often would they listen to him? Perhaps once, out of *curiosity*, but not again.

It is impossible, as I said already, to exert *influence upon legislation*; what for heaven's sake should then be the purpose of stating our principles in the "Reichstag"? Should it be perhaps to convert some of its members? To consider such a possibility would be more than naive, it would be childish.

It would be just as useful, and less ridiculous, to prattle about our principles to the billows of the sea. Fellows like Braun[16] and their associates know very well what we want. For them, as in general for *the ruling classes*, almost exclusively represented in the Reichstag, *socialism is no longer a question of theory, but simply a question of power, which, like any other question of power, cannot be decided in parliament, but only in the streets, on the battle-field.*

"Of course we do not hope to influence the 'Reichstag' itself, we wish to use the Reichstag platform to talk to the people outside."

Very well. At one time I also used the platform of the Reichstag in this way, and when the opportunity arises I will do so again. But is it the best place for theoretical elaboration? In the "Reichstag" the deputy is not permitted to read his speech and you will agree with me that even the most experienced orator – even gainsaying that his audience is listening quietly, which is certainly not the case in the "Reichstag" – cannot deliver a scientific discourse from memory and dictate it to the stenographers in so finished a form as he could write at his desk at home.

"But in the Reichstag he can state certain things that are banned elsewhere."

I deny that. In the "Reichstag" I can make attacks upon

the present *political* order, which would not pass unpunished in any other *Prussian* assembly, but with regard to *social* matters, particularly in the theoretical field, there is nothing that could not be said elsewhere with equal impunity. And should we fear to do battle with the law? The fact is that in Prussia far more revolutionary words are freely written and spoken every day than can be found on the social question in all the speeches delivered in the "Reichstag."

But let us assume that somebody succeeded in smuggling into the "Reichstag" a truth that could not have been uttered anywhere else – what has been gained thereby? The law undoubtedly permits the printing of the speech in question; however, if the press reproduces only *excerpts* from a speech or *one* speech only instead of *the entire debate*, the law makes the press *responsible for every single word* of the speech whether printed in full or in part. And even the largest newspapers, let alone the small Social-Democratic sheets, have not sufficient space to publish the authorized stenographic report of the *entire* debate.

The truth, so cleverly smuggled into the "Reichstag," can only be smuggled out again to the people by way of the official stenographic report; which however is inaccessible to the masses because of its volume and price.

What the workers learn of the debates dealing with social questions, they learn from the labour papers, and what the latter publish in the form of parliamentary reports, they could publish far better, much more carefully composed, in their own leading articles and essays.

I should also like to mention that the practical argument about "smuggling in" originates with those who are least likely to deal in any goods offending against the police regulations. Take for example the "great speech"[17] of Herr von Schweitzer – every word of it would have been passed by the pre-March censorship.

To sum up:

- Our speeches cannot exert any direct influence on legislation.
- Our speeches cannot convert the "Reichstag."
- Our speeches do not enable us to disseminate among the masses any truths, which could not be publicized much better by other means.

What "practical" purpose, therefore, have the speeches delivered in the "Reichstag"? None! But speaking without purpose is a fool's game.

Not a single advantage! And here, on the other hand, are the disadvantages: principles have been sacrificed, serious political struggle has been degraded to the level of a sham fight, the people have been deluded into thinking that Bismarck's "Reichstag" is qualified to solve the social question. – And we should take part in the parliamentary game for "practical reasons"? Only treachery or short-sightedness can make such an unreasonable demand.

The method which is correct in principle always proves to be the best in practice as well. Loyalty to one's principles is the best policy.

I do not wish to maintain thereby that the parliamentary fight must always and under all circumstances be rejected. In periods of chronic debility, when the blood circulates sluggishly through the body politic, when the crushed spirit of the people sees no hope of salvation for decades to come, in such periods it may be useful to keep alight in some parliament a little lamp of liberty, whose bright flame will penetrate the surrounding night.

And when the people, when the "workers' battalions" stand ready at the gates of parliament, then perhaps a word from the speaker's platform can, like an electric spark, start a blaze and give the signal for the liberating action.

But now we are, thank God, *no longer* in a state of chronic stagnation, and *alas not yet* on the eve of an action, emanating from the midst of the people.

I do not underestimate the importance of the spoken word. But in a period of crisis, when one world is dying and another world is coming into being, *the representatives of the people must be among the people.* For my part, I consider it not only more honourable but also more useful to speak at a meeting of honest workers than in that society of Junkers, apostates and nonentities, called the North German "Reichstag," which has been brought together at a nod from a statesman who despises both justice and humanity.

"But the Reichstag is the offspring of *universal suffrage.* Universal suffrage is the will of the people, and as democrats we must respect the will of the people, and consequently the Reichstag."

In this argument, which is fairly common, we encounter *the unreasonable overvaluation of universal suffrage,* which, based on Lassalle's authority, has developed into downright *idolatry.* Many people, particularly in North Germany, believe that universal suffrage is a magic wand, which will open to the "rited" the gates of state power; they labour under the delusion that though living in a police and military state they can pull themselves out of the quagmire of social misery by means of universal suffrage; as of yore *Münchhausen* pulled himself out by his pigtail. Their head should be graced by Münchhausen's queue. Universal suffrage is undoubtedly a "sacred right" of the people, a fundamental principle of the democratic, the Social-Democratic state. But by itself, separated from civil liberty, without freedom of the press, without freedom of association, subjected to the sabre of the policeman and soldier – in short, *in the absolutist state, universal suffrage can be nothing but the plaything and tool of absolutism.*

24

When Louis Bonaparte had assassinated the Republic, he proclaimed universal suffrage.

When Count Bismarck had enabled the particularism of the Prussian Junkers to triumph, when by his 1866 "successes" he had vanquished the liberal bourgeoisie in Prussia and had dismembered Germany, he did what his prototype had done fifteen years earlier, he proclaimed universal suffrage.

On both of these occasions the victory of despotism was sealed by the proclamation, the imposition of universal suffrage. This alone should be sufficient to open the eyes of the naive enthusiasts who worship the gospel of universal suffrage.

This is not the place to discuss Bonaparte's motives. As to Count Bismarck, his reasons are perfectly obvious.

The three-class election system[18], undemocratic and anti-democratic as it is, has at the same time an anti-feudal character, since it moves the centre of gravity within the parliamentary representation to the propertied classes. Although these classes are always ready to make common cause with absolutism against the workers, against democracy, they are, *nevertheless*, with the exception of the great landowners, *enemies of the absolutist state*, and to a certain degree they are "liberal."

The liberal Chamber of Deputies, the product of the three-class election system, was inconvenient to the Junker government. A counterbalance had to be established, this was achieved by means of universal, direct and equal suffrage.

How many persons can be found in the present-day police state; in the state of intellectual and military drill, who are intellectually and materially independent? The peasantry alone, which in this country obeys unquestioningly and has to obey every gesture of the authorities, constitutes fully two-thirds of the total population.

Count Bismarck counted on this and did not miscalculate. With the help of universal suffrage he swept away the opposition of the propertied classes and acquired a docile majority in the "Reichstag," which he could never have obtained under the three-class election system.

Hence universal suffrage was introduced not as a lever for democracy, but as a weapon for reaction.

It is entirely controlled by the government, in this country even more than in France, where the people are politically more experienced, where they have already gone through three revolutions and are facing the fourth. It is quite safe to say that in Prussia no one can be elected to the "Reichstag," whom the government *seriously opposes*. I recall how during the last elections in Hanover the proclamations issued by the opposition were confiscated and thousands of obstacles placed in its way. And in this case a candidate was involved who was merely *inconvenient*, not *dangerous*. Had the government used all its power – I mean used it *lawfully*, for the "intelligent" absolutism usually hides behind a legal cloak – it could have easily prevented Ewald's[19] election. Suppose that a candidate is nominated, whom the government definitely wants to keep out of the "Reichstag": it will confiscate the newspapers which support his election – quite legally; it will seize his election circulars – again legally; it will prohibit election campaign meetings – legally; or it may permit such meetings and then dissolve them – also legally; it will arrest the candidate's sponsors – legally; it will arrest the candidate himself – perfectly legally. Even a "member of the Reichstag" was recently arrested, and today he would still have been in prison had not a gesture from Bismarck convinced the National-Liberals of the "martyr's" inoffensiveness.

But assuming that a feeling of confidence or some miscalculation caused the government to refrain from using its powers, and that we succeeded in electing to the "Reichstag" a Social-Democratic majority, which is the dream of some fanciful Socialist politicians – what should the majority do? *Hic Rhodus, hic salta*. Now is the moment to transform society and the state. The majority adopts an epoch-making resolution, a new era is born-by no means; a company of soldiers drives the Social-Democratic majority from the sanctuary and if these gentlemen do not submit quietly, they are escorted by a few policemen to the city jail where they have time to meditate on their quixotic conduct.

Revolutions are not made with the gracious permission of the authorities; the socialist ideal cannot be accomplished within the present state; it can be brought into existence only by overthrowing the existing state.

No peace with the present-day state.

Away with the cult of the universal and direct suffrage.

Let us continue to participate actively in the elections, using them however merely as *means of propaganda*, and emphasizing always that the ballot-box can never become the cradle of the democratic state. Universal suffrage will acquire its decisive influence on the state and society only *after* the abolition of the police and military state.

Finally a word on the various kinds of socialism, which we now encounter in Germany, and also in the "Reichstag," and which correspond closely to our *political* party structure.

First we have – for I need not speak here of Dr. Max Hirsch[20] who claims that class contradictions are a "misapprehension" and who acts, so to speak, as a voluntary special constable of the bourgeoisie against socialism – first we have *the royal Prussian court socialism* or *feudal socialism*, as represented by Herr Wagener who incidentally adapted the machinery of universal suffrage for Count Bismarck. Numerous facts are available to prove that Herr Wagener does not carry on socialism on his own responsibility, but acts on instructions from above. I need only remind you of the tolerance shown by the police towards the General Association of German Workers, which had been declared "unlawful" by the Supreme Court. Two more facts, which are not widely known, may be cited.

When the **Norddeutsche Allgemeine Zeitung**[21] entered

into that well-known relationship with Count Bismarck, as a consequence of which I had to withdraw from the paper, *Brass*[22] *offered to place two columns daily in his sheet at the disposal of Marx, Engels and myself,* remarking that *we could write on socialism and communism without restriction. The government, in which we were mistaken, intended to do something for the poor man, for the proletariat.* Of course I declined; we cannot assist in placing the labour movement in the hands of royalty by divine grace.

By the way, this happened *before* the publication of Lassalle's reply[23], proving that the government was not induced by Lassalle to study the social question, an allegation frequently made by both his friends and his enemies.

The second fact: During a meeting of the Committee for the Relief of Distress in East Prussia, a Progressive member complained that official and semi-official circles were flirting with certain socialist aspirations. Whereupon the second highest person in the state – that is, if one does not consider Count Bismarck to be the highest person – to whom the remark had been addressed (the crown prince), declared: "*This is the express wish of Count Bismarck who is of the opinion that encouragement of socialist aspirations is the best way to paralyse democracy.*"

Secondly, we have *the National-Liberal* Socialists, who base themselves on the "conditions created in 1866," who accept the *coup d'etat*, consider that the constitution of the North German Separate Federation can be improved and endeavour to improve it. Like the National-Liberal practical *politicians*, the National-Liberal practical *Socialists* – in so far as they are honest – are happily blessed with the simple faith, that in spite of all their compromises they can keep their principles pure and that in the end they will manage to outwit the police and military state. The miserable failure suffered by Braun, Miquel[24] and their associates is a portent of their fate. The inconsistency of this political view is clearly revealed by the fact that the National-Liberal Socialists are acting in perfect unison *politically* with the National-Liberal bourgeoisie, whose social rule they wish to break.

Democratic socialism has nothing in common either with this National-Liberal or that feudal socialism, both of which rest on the separation of the social from the political question. Democratic socialism proceeds from the principle that the political and social questions are inseparable; proudly rejecting any pact with the existing order, it is determined to win a democratic state for a society that will be organized on a socialist basis. Only we, the adherents of *this* socialism, are justified in calling ourselves a socialist *party*. The others are a clique or a sect. *We are Social-Democracy.*

We are not suspended in mid-air, as some people allege, we merely have nothing in common with the present order of things, neither politically nor socially. I am a *republican*, the fact that I live in a monarchy, does not make me a royalist.

We do recognize power, but only as *a fact*, not as a right – as a fact which we endure until this power will no longer have power, that is, until it can be opposed by a greater power. We do not sit idle, but we use all the weapons, left us by the ruling power, to fight the ruling power. And thus "we are also acting according to circumstances" – in the only manner consistent with our principles and with good sense.

French democracy provides us with a brilliant example. Having made his *coup d'etat*, Bonaparte proclaimed universal suffrage and built a golden bridge designed to span the river of blood spilled on December 2 and lead across to democracy, to the people, to the workers.

French democracy – let it be said to its immortal glory – scornfully rejected the allurements offered by the emperor, remaining faithful to its principles, faithful to its hatred. Eighteen years have passed; those few, who, like *Ollivier*, could not resist the magic of success and have crossed the golden bridge, bear the mark of Cain's treachery on their forehead and are shunned by every honest person, while *French democracy faces Caesarism solidly, uncompromisingly, confident of victory, certain of victory.*

Neither will we cross the golden bridge, we are biding our time, and letting the may-flies hatched by the sun of "success" die.

We cannot prevent the government's attempts to exploit the labour question, but we can and will ensure that those attempts fail; we can and will prevent reaction, the Junkers from benefiting by the class struggle between proletariat and bourgeoisie. We will succeed in this if we wage the *political* struggle as vigorously as we do the social struggle. I know that in Prussia this is difficult, but it *must* be done. First of all the working class must rid itself of the distrust, artificially produced and kept alive, against so-called "bourgeois democracy," which is represented by *Jacoby.*

If someone wishes to spread confusion among the parties, he only needs to fling a *double-entendre*, an ambiguous expression, among them. "Bourgeois democracy" is such an expression, such an apple of discord.

The word "bourgeois" (*Bürger*) in German has three different meanings. First, it means *citizen*, and in this sense it comprises the idea of political equality; secondly, it means *the petty bourgeois*, and the conditions of the petty bourgeoisie in Germany compel it in its own interest to side with the working class; thirdly, and finally, it means the bourgeois, the *big bourgeois* who lives by the exploitation of workers and seeks to perpetuate it.

Because of the hateful associations connected with the word "bourgeois," the expression "bourgeois democracy" has become a term of abuse for many workers. But is the bourgeoisie democratic? On the contrary. It is well aware of the close connection existing between democracy and socialism, it hates democracy and is *national-liberal*. And strange to relate, the same people who with passionate fury attack Jacoby, *the enemy of the bourgeoisie*, as a "bourgeois democrat," are *politically* hand in glove with the bourgeoisie and help it to uphold *its social privileges. This proves that those who shout against "bourgeois democracy" are either very short-sighted or very dishonest.*

Jacoby, I admit, is not yet a socialist in the strict sense of the word. He still emphasizes the political aspect more than the social aspect, which is just as serious an error as the reverse. But as surely as he values truth and justice above everything, so surely will he come over to us entirely. Even though he is still more of a politician than a socialist, that shall not deter us from accepting the proffered hand. *We do not wish to quarrel with our friends about minor questions for the benefit of our enemies. The future belongs to the socialism which is democratic, to the democracy which is socialist.*

In March 1848 all were democrats. When the movement, however, became serious and it became evident that either the "achievements" would be lost, or a real complete revolution had to be made giving the proletariat its rights, the democratic bourgeoisie, or, to use a more accurate term, the democratizing" bourgeoisie, madly frightened by the spectre of communism, separated from the democratic working class. Where now are the bourgeois democrats of those day? The "old democrats," the "men of 1848," have not *fallen away*, as has been often claimed, they have merely fallen into the place where they belonged, where they were due to fall. From unconscious bourgeois they turned into conscious bourgeois, as soon as the economic contradictions developed, in consequence of the enormous industrial and commercial upsurge after 1848. So far as they are not dead and gone, today we find those democratic bourgeois almost without exception in the ranks of the more or less progressive National-Liberalism; they were *never democrats* but merely muddle-heads intoxicated by democratic phrases, the content of which they did not understand.

The true democrat is of necessity a socialist as well.

A more determined position than they occupied so far ought to be taken up in the social sphere by the democrats, which are represented by Jacoby, and in the political sphere by the Socialists. Only when that is done, when socialist and democratic efforts strengthen and complement each other instead of fighting one another, will a broad and powerful social-democratic movement come into being, strong enough to break down any resistance confronting it.

Why is Social-Democracy at present still so weak? I am fully aware that much noise is made about it, but it is great boast and small roast. Having the advantage of looking behind the scenes I consider it very foolish-leaving the moral issue completely aside-to try to deceive the public and our own party about our strength. But why is our party at present so weak? *Why does the overwhelming majority of the workers keep aloof?* Why does Social-Democracy particularly in Berlin apparently have such a small following? Only quite recently, as a result of a successful strike[25], has it been able to unite under its banner a few hundred men. A few hundred out of a hundred thousand!

Why? The conviction that at present the reactionary forces are taking advantage of the social movement, that they benefit by it, this *well-founded* conviction keeps away the masses, who possess democratic instincts.

When all uncertainty regarding the political position of Social-Democracy is removed, when Social-Democracy without neglecting the class struggle stands in the forefront of the political fight, from that moment onwards we will have the backing of the working masses and will be able to say: "Berlin belongs to us." And then Germany will belong to us; for the chief enemy is here in Berlin, and the decisive battle will be fought here. Germany was enslaved from Berlin, and Germany must be liberated in Berlin.

* * *

The speech was followed by an animated discussion. Commenting upon the observations made by a member of the General Association of German Workers (Herr Armborst) Liebknecht said *inter alia*:

"The arguments of the previous speaker demonstrate where an attempt to separate socialism from democracy leads; for him democrat is synonymous with bourgeois, according to this logic the worker must of course be a reactionary.

"I thought I had proved that I fear neither the laughter nor the howls of rage of the gentlemen in the 'Reichstag.' I may say that I have defied them as no one has; but I did it to protest, to state my opinion of the 'Reichstag' and everything connected with it, and one cannot do that often. Otherwise it loses its value. To preach socialist theories *pour le roi de Prusse* to the benches of the 'Reichstag,' I feel beneath my dignity.

"I have not the least intention of conducting the actual fight in the political field only. Even in 1864 I publicly advocated *trade unions*, and I did my utmost since then to organize them. But here too one should never lose sight of the ultimate goal, of the principle. For if that happens it is only too easy to forget, in the struggle for material improvements, for higher wages, *that the bourgeois mode of production in its entirety has to be reorganized, that the wage system as a whole must be abolished.*

"One final word. Herr Armborst believes that in time we would gain a majority in the 'Reichstag.' Let him consider the following calculation: at present we have even 'Social-Democrats' in the 'Reichstag'; provided that at the next and each of the following elections we get seven more – and that is certainly a most *favourable* supposition – 63 years must elapse, before we obtain in this way the majority, that is, at least 149 deputies for the 'Reichstag' has 297 members. Well, if Herr

Armborst and his friends feel inclined to wait until the elections of 1933, they may do so; we consider it a crime against Social-Democracy *to hold the workers back from the political struggle, waged at the present time, by holding out hopes for the future.*"

TRAGI-COMIC SEQUEL

Habent sua fata libelli [Books have their fate (Latin)].

Not only books, but speeches too have their strange fate. At any rate the preceding speech. I had already forgotten all about it when one fine morning in August 1869 the postman delivered an epistle bearing a Berlin postmark. Its antediluvian size and its garb of greyish brown blotting-paper immediately betrayed its official origin. My curiosity aroused, I opened the object and read that a *Mr. Schütz*, royal Prussian public prosecutor, had made a study of the speech in question and claimed to have discovered in it a "defamation of the royal Prussian Government." According to the notes taken by the various police officers of higher and lower rank, who had honoured the meeting of May 31 with their presence, I am supposed to have said among other things:

"Germany's present political structure exists only through a violation of law, and is upheld by the sword."

Whether I used these particular expressions, I can no longer recall, but similar ones certainly, when I compared Bismarck's *coup d'etat* with the December *coup* of Bonaparte. In any case as official representative of the Prussian *constitutional* state – *in partibus* – Mr. Schütz was scandalized by the expression "violation of law"; moreover, in his legal zeal he so completely forgot his character as a citizen of the Prussian *military* state *in esse* that to be "upheld by the *sword*" seemed to him also a criminal offence. To do justice to the man, I will however not exclude the possibility of his wrath being caused by the error I committed in confusing the old heathen and medieval "sword" with the modern champion of civilization, the "needle-gun," which does indeed show my great ignorance in military matters. However that may be, Mr. Schütz has attended the compulsory course of lectures in logic and felt obliged to testify to this with the following argument: "Germany's present political structure has been brought about by the policy of the Prussian Government, it is *therefore* a defamation of this policy to identify it with a violation of the law." This could also be formulated thus: "Germany's present political structure rests on the policy of *the Prussian Government*, the Prussian Government can do no wrong, violation of the law is a wrong, it is *therefore* a defamation of the Prussian Government to identify it with a violation of the law." Or: "The Prussian Government *violated* the law in 1866 and that was *right*; *to say*, however, that it violated the law," is wrong. Liebknecht said it, *therefore* he must be punished." On the basis of this logical argument Mr. Schütz had filed an application with the Berlin City Court, to order an investigation against me for infringement of §101 ("hatred and contempt"). The City Court, whose members had also studied the *collegium logicum*, notified me in the greyish-brown blotting-paper epistle, that I must present myself for a hearing at the premises of the Berlin City Court, Lagerhaus, Klostergasse 76, first floor, at 10:45 a.m. on September 17, 1869. "If you do not appear," threatened the epistle, "the court as it sees fit will proceed to hear evidence and to pass and pronounce the judgement in contumacy, or it will fix another hearing and order you to be *arrested and brought before it*." That sounded rather businesslike: "arrest," "bring before" – I felt a cold shiver and I experienced again the familiar smell of bugs which pervades the city jail – but luckily I remembered the old saying, that in Nuremberg they cannot hang anybody before catching him, and praising the Creator for the fact that Saxony had not yet been completely "annexed," I threw the greyish-brown blotting-paper epistle in with the rest of the editorial waste paper, packed my travelling bag and cheerfully set out for the International Congress at Basle.

Again I forgot the Berlin speech and the greyishbrown blotting-paper epistle. However the City Court of Berlin had a better memory. Approximately two weeks after my return from

Basle, the postman delivered a second greyish-brown blotting-paper epistle. Its outside resembled the first as closely as one infantry helmet resembles another, – but inside it differed slightly. But the intentional or unintentional humour remained the same. Epistle No.2 reads as follows:

IN THE NAME OF THE KING

In the lawsuit against the writer Wilhelm Martin Philipp Christian Ludwig Liebknecht Lit. L., No. 35 de 1869 the Royal City Court at Berlin, division of lawsuits, section VII offences, in its session of September 17, 1869 at which the following took part:

Meisner, judge at the City Court, presiding, and Assistant Judges: Count von Bredow, Klingner passed the following judgement in accordance with the oral proceedings:

that the defendant, the writer Wilhelm Martin Philipp Christian Ludwig Liebknecht is guilty of defamation of government instructions and is therefore to be sentenced to three months imprisonment, and he is to defray the costs of the proceedings.

ACCORDING TO THE LAW
Reasons

Against the defendant, the writer Wilhelm Martin Philipp Christian Ludwig Liebknecht, born on March 29, 1826, domiciled in Leipzig, legally sentenced by the Royal City Court in Berlin on October 19, 1866 to three months imprisonment for returning without permission after having been banished from the country; duly summoned to the case hearings, but failing to appear, without being excused, and therefore to be dealt with in contumacy according to §51 of the decree issued on January 3, 1849, it is regarded as proved on the basis of the evidence given on official oath by police captain Beyer and police lieutenant

Liedtke:

that on May 31, 1869 a public meeting of the Democratic Workers' Association took place on the premises of Engelhard on Lindenstrasse in Berlin, for the police supervision of which the two above-mentioned witnesses were detailed; that the defendant delivered an address there on the political position of Social-Democracy, in the course of which the defendant stated that Count Bismarck made a *coup d'etat* in Germany, just as Napoleon had done in France, and that finally the defendant followed this up with the verbatim remark: "*Germany's present political structure exists only through a violation of the law, and is upheld by the sword.*"

Considering the fact that the defendant undoubtedly understands by the name "Bismarck" not this statesman alone and personally, but rather the Prussian policy, which emanates from and is directed by the same and is approved by the government; considering further that this policy and the action of the Prussian Government brought about Germany's present political structure, that consequently the defendant therefore identified the Prussian policy with a violation of the law, alleging that right is not its basis, but the power of the sword, the court could not doubt, and deemed it as *actually established*:

that on May 31, 1869, in Berlin, the defendant publicly defamed and exposed *the orders of the government to hatred.*

The defendant is thus guilty of an offence within the meaning of §101 of the penal code.

Taking into account that the statement was made by the defendant in a public meeting, organized by an association, and that it is very likely to weaken and impair the prestige and authority of the government, *particularly among politically less educated persons*, the court deemed it appropriate to sentence him to *three months* imprisonment. In accordance with §17S of the decree of January 3, 1849, the defendant has to defray the costs of the proceedings.

This document has been duly drawn up, signed, and the seal of the Royal City Court has been affixed to it.

Berlin, September 17, 1869.
Royal City Court.
Division of Lawsuits.
Section 7 Offences.
Ficker.
Meisner.
(l.s.)

* * *

I leave the criticism of the sentence to the *Kladderadatsch*[26], as soon as it has dropped its lackey's livery and regained its wit. It is true that among the "politically less (than Schütz, Meisner, Bredow and Klingner) educated persons" of whom my audience consisted, there was hardly one, who could have handled logic and common sense as ingeniously as did Schütz, Meisner, Bredow and Klingner. The reasoning in support of the sentence shows in any case that there is not only "humour in the dock" but also "humour in the judge's seat." Had I called Bismarck an enthusiast of right and justice, the dismemberment of Germany – a lawful act, the sword – a needle-gun or a breech-loader manufactured by Krupp, and the battle of Sadowa[27] – a tender love-affair – the merry "judges of Berlin" would have recommended me for the next Birthday Honours List, instead of sentencing me to three months in contumacy.

But the mere sentencing did not satisfy them, the joke had to be carried into effect. To "crown the work" I had to serve the three months. The men of Nuremberg, I wanted to say of Berlin, therefore applied for my extradition to the authorities in Leipzig; they were however informed that such practical jokes were not appreciated in Saxony. Whereupon they declared, somewhat subdued by the rebuff, that they would be satisfied if I were to be sent to a prison in Saxony for three months by means of the joint whip, *the Law on Legal Redress*. But a little mishap occurred: they had forgotten *to read* the law to which they referred. Nevertheless the new joke was more to the taste of their colleagues in Leipzig. I soon noticed that the local district court felt disposed to incorporate me, and behold, a decision to that effect was adopted. My solicitor and friend, Freytag, sent the following protest in my name against this highly unwelcome attempted annexation:

TO THE ROYAL COURT OF JUDICATURE AT THE DISTRICT COURT IN LEIPZIG

The Royal City Court in Berlin has requested the Royal Court of Judicature here to make me serve a sentence of three months imprisonment, which the named city court had imposed upon me for alleged defamation of government orders.

It is quite incomprehensible that the Royal Court of Judicature should have decided to comply with this demand.

Against the validity of the proceedings of the Royal City Court and the Royal Court of Judicature, I submit the following:

1. The offence which I am alleged to have committed would be a political offence, so that existing legal provisions regarding extradition, imprisonment, etc. must be rigorously interpreted.

2. According to enclosures A and B I have been accused of and sentenced for an offence against §101 of the Prussian penal code and in particular because I had by public defamation exposed *government orders to hatred.*

This is however not a punishable offence according to the legislation of Saxony since penal code abolished the so-called "hatred and contempt paragraph."

3. According to Article 35, of the Saxon-Prussian Convention of the November 30, 1839, which was not repealed by the Confederation Law on Legal Redress but was on the contrary confirmed by §46 of this law, criminals and other law offenders are not to be handed over by the state to which they belong but are to be tried and punished there for offences committed in the other state. *Therefore they cannot be tried in contumacy in the other state.*

According to enclosure B the Prussian City Court now demands that the authorities in Saxony put into effect a judgement based on a contumacy procedure which in my case is unlawful.

Article 36 of the above-mentioned convention is not applicable, and proves on the contrary how unjustifiable is the request of the Berlin City Court.

4. In conformity with §25 of the Confederation Law on Legal Redress, extradition does *not* take place if the action in question is a political offence or if it is not liable to punishment according to the law of the federal state on whose territory the convicted person resides.

In my case both these conditions are fulfilled. §27 of this law reads:

If in conformity with the provisions made in §25, Nos. 1 and 3, an extradition does not take place, the defendant is to be tried for the actions he is charged with in the state in which he lives and before the court of the district in which he dwells, provided the laws of this state make no other stipulation as to the competency of the court; thus stating again, and thereby corroborating further Article 35 of the convention already quoted, that a contumacy procedure against me was *inadmissible* in connection with the offence I am alleged to have committed; that no Saxon court has any right to execute the sentence passed against me on the basis of such a procedure; and that it is to be left to the Royal Prussian Procurator's Office to file an application against me with the competent authority, the Royal Court of Judicature at the Leipzig District Court.

5.The above propositions are quite clear and are based on an undoubtedly correct interpretation of the existing legislation.

But even if one were to assume that Prussian courts were entitled to sentence in contumacy inhabitants of Saxony for political offences and for actions that are not punishable in Saxony, and that the Saxon courts were obliged to execute such sentences, §33 of the above-mentioned federal law nevertheless stipulates that the courts in one federal state are obliged only to carry out the sentence passed in another federal state, if the sentence is a fine or imprisonment not exceeding four weeks, not therefore in my case where a sentence of three months imprisonment is involved.

Under the circumstances I consider my objection to the proceedings of the Berlin City Court and the Royal Court of Judicature to be fully justified, and I request the later to reject the application made by the Royal City Court referring it to the existing laws. Should, however, the Royal Court of Judicature not comply with my request. I lodge herewith a complaint against it, and request that in that event my legal council – the author of this protest, whom I give herewith full power of attorney to safeguard my rights – should be informed of the forwarding of this case to the higher authorities.

Leipzig, October 18, 1869.
Wilhelm Liebknecht

* * *

The protest was effective: the decision of the court in Leipzig was annulled and the Berlin City Court was firmly advised that it had read something *into* the Law on Legal

Redress that ordinary eyes could not *discern* there.

That is not yet the end of the matter. The best is still to come.

The "humour in the judge's seat" which had miscarried found an avenger, and a high and mighty one at that, in the shape of *the Prussian Government*, which represents in this tragi-comic affair the tragic element, *sit venia verbo*. A mystical darkness surrounds the subsequent events, and both Berlin and Dresden are equally interested in preserving it. The only positive facts are:

> 1. *that the Prussian Government requested the Government of Saxony to try me for defamation of the institutions of the Confederation, because I had publicly declared that they were brought about by a violation of the law and by violence.*

And it is certain

> 2. *that the Government of Saxony complied with this request and gave orders to initiate proceedings against me, as desired in Berlin.*

Never, I dare say, has one government made a more impudent demand on another government, and never has one government made a more humiliating concession to another.

Just imagine: in 1866 Saxony sided with the German Confederation[28] and Austria, Saxon troops fought side by side with the Austrians against the Prussians, and because the Saxon Government considered Prussia's action a violation of the law and would not tolerate it, its soldiers were shot down at Gitschin[29] by Prussians at the command of the Prussian Government.

And this same Prussian Government expected this same Saxon Government to prosecute the mere statement of this fact!

And the Saxon Government did it! In its *new-found* loyalty towards the Confederation the Saxon Government went so far as to stamp *old* loyalty towards the Confederation as a crime, a crime so serious that criminal action had to be brought even against the simple assertion that its victorious enemy of 1866 had at the time been in the wrong and itself in the right.

Subsequently they may have noticed in Dresden how strange the procedure was; the fact is that the trial, nominally conducted against me, but in reality by the Saxon Government *against itself, that is, by the Saxon Government of 1870 against the Saxon Government of 1866*, soon came to a standstill and showed shadowy signs of life only two or three times at long intervals apart, till finally it merged in the celebrated "high treason trial," which offered the best opportunity (fully exploited by the manufacturers of air-bricks *à la* Münchhausen) for using the "Berlin speech." But that does not concern us here.

Farewell, dear reader, and I hope you will be edified by the specimen of contemporary history, which I presented to you. And finally my thanks to the merry wags of Berlin, the priceless quadruplet: *Schutz, Meisner, Bredow and Klingner,* for the amusing episode in the midst of more serious fighting. Though admittedly it is not too serious. Our most serious fights are still comparatively rather cosy. Beyond the Rhine is *Satory*[30], on this side only *Hubertusburg*. Or, so far only Hubertusburg[31]?

> Leipzig, June 7, 1872,
> in the prison of the district court
> *W. Liebknecht*

EPILOGUE
[to the London Edition of 1889]

My last remark in the debate was aimed at the opinion, still widespread at the time but now fortunately extinct, that the assiduous use of universal suffrage would in the near future yield the workers *a majority in the Reichstag.* The calculation I gave as an example works out even more unfavourably for the *German Reichstag* which consists of 397 members, than it did for the *North German Reichstag* with its 297 members.

Under present circumstances – and this has to be emphasized as strongly as possible – *it is inconceivable that Social-Democracy might obtain a majority in parliament.* The conditions for that *have as yet to be created*; and we *can* create them only by winning over the masses to our point of view through *agitation* and *propaganda*, and through *organization make our forces effective.* For us parliamentary activity is not an *end*, but only the *means to an end* – it must assist us *outside the Reichstag, to win* such influence with *the people* that *Legislation will not be able to turn away the justified demands of the working class.*

To *Johann Jacoby*, who was mentioned in my speech, I owe the explanation, that *two years later*, when *Bebel* and I had been sentenced to two years imprisonment in a fortress for an act of "high treason" which we had never committed, Jacoby declared himself publicly and without reservations an adherent and *a member of the Social-Democratic Party.*

What I said about *the petty bourgeoisie*, today seems no longer quite appropriate, because the German petty bourgeoisie has flocked in large numbers to Ackermann's banner of guild and fossilized periwig. Well, that is a transient mental disease from which the people will recover as soon as they make the

45

inevitable discovery that the magic medicine dispensed by the social quacks merely aggravates the malady and *accelerates the process of proletarization.*

The final sentence of my speech gives me particular satisfaction. What I had then *hoped* for, has *come to pass* to an extent exceeding all expectations. Today nobody can regard any longer as a "futile boast" the statement: *"Berlin belongs to us!"*

We see our goal before us in the immediate future. Looking back to 1869, we realize the enormous progress we have made and *how rapidly we are advancing – for all that.* And our pace will not slacken. On the contrary. The further *the avalanche advances, the faster it moves, and the easier it overcomes any resistance.*

December 1888.
W. Liebknecht

Notes

1. *North German Confederation* – a federal state, formed after the Austro-Prussian War of 1866. It comprised 19 German states and three free cities with a population of 30 million. Prussia dominated the Confederation.

2. *Bismarck, Otto, von Schonhausen, Prince* (1815-1898) – reactionary Prussian and German statesman, head of the Prussian government from 1862, first chancellor of the German Empire from 1871 to 1890; organizer of Germany's unification which was accomplished by counter-revolutionary methods under Prussia's hegemony; a vehement enemy of the labour movement, he introduced the Anti-Socialist Law

3. *High treason trial at Leipzig* – Legal proceedings instituted by the government against Wilhelm Liebknecht, August Bebel, and Adolf Hepner, who publicly opposed annexation of Alsace and Lorraine after the Franco-Prussian War. At the trial which took place in March 1872 Liebknecht and Bebel were sentenced to two years imprisonment.

4. *Augean stables* – in Greek mythology the legendary king Augeas' stables not cleaned for 30 years and which the hero Hercules cleansed in one day; synonym for extreme filth and corruption.

5. *August Bebel* (1840-1913) – one of the founders and a prominent figure of the German Social-Democratic Party and of the Second International, friend of Marx and Engels, ardent opponent of revisionist tendencies. Towards the end of his life he held centrist views on a number of questions.

6. *General Association of German Workers* – the first political workers' organization covering the whole of Germany founded in 1863. Its first president was F. Lasalle, after his death actual leadership was taken over by Schweitzer. The Association which followed an opportunist policy on many questions

existed till 1875 when it united at the Gotha Congress with the Social-Democratic Workers' Party of Germany (Eisenachers) led by Bebel and Liebknecht, to form the Socialist Workers' Party of Germany.

7. *Schweitzer, Johann Baptist von* (1833-1875) – German lawyer, journalist and writer one of the closest collaborators of Lassalle and advocate of his views; from 1867 to 1871 president of the General Association of German Workers. He pursued a policy of collaboration with Bismarck's Government, which Marx and Engels called "royal Prussian socialism." In 1872 he was expelled from the Association after disclosure of his connections with the Prussian authorities.

8. *Jacoby, Johann* (1805-1877) – German publicist and politician, bourgeois democrat. In 1848 a leader of the Left in the Prussian National Assembly; during the 60s a Left Progressive and active opponent of Bismarck. He joined the Social-Democratic Workers' Party in 1872, his views however, remaining those of a left bourgeois democrat.

9. ***Demokratisches Wochenblatt*** – a periodical published in Leipzig in 1868-1869 and edited by W. Liebknecht; it was the organ of the People's Party and the Union of Workers' Societies and subsequently of the Social-Democratic Workers' Party (Eisenachers.)

10. *Wagener, Hermann* (1815-1889) – German reactionary politician and publicist, one of Bismarck's closest collaborators, an advocate of so-called state socialism.

11. *Ketteler, Wilhelm-Emanuel* – Baron, from 1850 Bishop of Mainz. Author of **The Labour Problem and Christianity** and other works on social and political questions, founder of the reactionary "Christian socialism" in Germany. In the early 70s he was a member of the Reichstag and influential in the Centre Party.

12. *Prussian constitutional conflict* – conflict between the Prussian king and government on one side, and the majority of

the Landtag, consisting of the Progressive Party and some of the Liberals, on the other. In 1861 the government proposed in the Landtag to reorganize the army and lengthen military service; the majority of the Landtag opposed extension of military service and demanded control over budgetary expenditure refusing to pass the budget if this were not granted. The government carried out the military reform and continued its expenditures without Landtag approval. The conflict lasted over five years. After the Austro-Prussian War and the formation of the North German Confederation it ended with the complete retreat of the Landtag majority, which confirmed the government expenditure by antedating its approval for the whole period of the conflict.

13. *Fortschrittspartei (Progressive Party)* – voiced the interests of a considerable section of the German bourgeoisie; founded in 1861 by Virchow, the scientist, and Schultze-Delitzsch, proponent of co-operative societies. It advocated Germany's unification under Prussian hegemony, revision of industrial legislation, reorganization of the Upper House, formation of a responsible cabinet and local administrative reforms. Up to the establishment of the North German Confederation the party was very influential, but after the Austro-Prussian war a large section broke away to form the National-Liberal Party.

14. *Blood and iron policy* – thus Bismarck described his German unification policy in a speech delivered before the Prussian Landtag in 1862.

15. *Lasalle, Ferdinand* (1825-64) – German petty-bourgeois writer and lawyer who joined the labour movement; a founder of the General Association of German Workers and its first president; supported the unification of Germany from above under Prussia's hegemony and ushered in opportunist trends in German Social-Democracy.

16. *Braun, Karl* (1822-1893) – reactionary German politician and publicist, from 1867 to 1887 member of the Reichstag and the Prussian Chamber of Representatives, belonged to the

National-Liberals, party of the big bourgeoisie.

17. *Von Schweitzer's "great speech"* – a reference to a speech made by Schweitzer, president of the General Association of German Workers, in the Reichstag of the North German Confederation on March 17, 1869, during the debate on craft regulations.

18. *Three-class election system* – the system regulating the elections to the Prussian Landtag from 1849-1918. It divided all voters into three classes in accordance with taxes paid. The total amount of taxes collected from the population was divided into three equal parts; a list of tax-payers compiled, beginning with those who paying the largest amounts. The first class, comprising the richest, was the smallest; the second, or less well-to-do was more numerous; and the third class, making up the rest, was largest. However, each of these classes elected an equal amount of electors, who in turn chose the deputies. The elections were therefore decided almost exclusively by the wealthy sectors, the propertied classes. Those who did not pay taxes had no right to vote.

19. *Ewald, Heinrich* (1803-1875) – German orientalist and well-known public figure, supporter of the Hanoverian Separatist Party (The Guelphs) and an opponent of Germany's unification under Prussian leadership, member of Reichstag.

20. *Hirsch, Max* (1832-1905) – German bourgeois economist, member of the Progressive Party, who (together with F. G. Duncker) founded the so-called Hirsch-Duncker trade unions, which preached class peace, endeavoured to place trade the trade-union movment under the control of the bourgeoisie and to prevent the spread of Marxist ideas among the workers.

21. **Norddeutsche Allgemeine Zeitung** (abbreviated **Norddeutsche**) – German daily published in Berlin from 1861 to 1918. During the first year of its existence the paper followed a bourgeois-democratic policy, during which period Liebknecht was one of its contributors. In 1862, it was taken over by

reactionary circles and up to 1890 subsidized by Bismarck.

22. *Brass, August* (1818-1876) – German publicist, during the revolutionary period of 1848-1849 a bourgeois democrat; founder and first editor of **Norddeutsche Allgemeine Zeitung** (till 1871); in 1862 joined the conservative camp and became an ardent supporter of Bismarck.

23. *Lassalle's reply* – a reference to the *Open Letter* in reply to the address of the Leipzig Committee of Workers' Education Societies requesting him to set forth his views on basic tasks facing the working class. His reply of March 1, 1863 proposed the establishment of an all-German workers' organization which was to fight for introducing universal suffrage by peaceful means.

24. *Miquel, Johannes* (1828-1901) – German bourgeois politician and statesman, a left democrat during the revolution of 1848, subsequently switched to the reactionary camp becoming a leader of the National-Liberal Party; several times re-elected to the Reichstag; in 1890-1901 he was Prussian Minister of Finance.

25. *Successful strike* – a reference to the carpenters' strike in Berlin in spring 1868 ending in a workers' victory.

26. **Kladderadatsch** – German satirical weekly founded in 1848. During the first years of its existence it scoffed at the old semi-feudal customs, but later it was taken over by reactionary circles and patronized by Bismarck.

27. *Battle of Sadowa* – largest military action of Austro-Prussian war of 1866, ended with the Austrian army's defeat and decided the war in Prussia's favour.

28. *German Confederation* – a union of 29 German states set up by the Vienna Congress in 1815. Austria played the leading rule; during the Austro-Prussian War many member states of the German Confederation fought on Austria's side.

29. *Battle of Gitschin (Jicin)* – an encounter between the

Prussian forces and those of Austria's ally Prince Albert of Saxony, near the town of Gitschin (Jicin) in Bohemia in 1866, which ended in the defeat and subsequent retreat of the Austrian and Saxon troops.

30. *Satory* – a prison near Versailles, where savage executions of the Paris Communards took place in 1871.

31. *Hubertusburg* – a prison in which Bebel and Liebknecht served their sentence after having been convicted in the Leipzig trial of 1872 (see note 3).